So, What Now?

Having received Jesus Christ as my Savior and Lord, what do I do to grow in my faith?

Copyright by Steve Boyd
First Edition

All rights reserved. No part of this book shall be reproduced, stored in a retrieval system, or transmitted by any means without written permission from the author.

ISBN-13: 978-0692491065
ISBN-10: 0692491066
Library of Congress Control Number: 2015947212
Publisher: Steve Boyd, Harrisburg, NC

Printed by CreateSpace, an Amazon.com Company

Dedication

I dedicate this book to all my family, but especially to my five grandchildren Dakota, Mona, Brook, Evan and Liam. It is my prayer that they would each discover these truths for themselves and choose to dedicate their lives to the Lord, serving Him in truth all the days of their lives. May the power of the Holy Spirit guide them in truth and joy, and direct their paths in all they do until Jesus returns.

In Loving Memory of

- Robert "Bob" James Cronin
- Dewey Lester Lail

Fellow Iron Men and brothers in the Lord who both transitioned from this life in 2014 and are now in the presence of our Lord Jesus Christ.

You both received your perfect healing, brothers, and I look forward to fellowship with you again for eternity.

Contents

	Page
Introduction	1
Chapter 1 – Responding to God	3
Chapter 2 – Prayer Principles	11
Chapter 3 – Bible Blessings	29
Chapter 4 – Wonders of Worship	41
Chapter 5 – Fellowship and Fun	53
Chapter 6 – Influencing Others	63
Chapter 7 – Seasons of Life	71
Chapter 8 - Just In Case	81
Appendix	83
Steps to Salvation	85
Bibliography	87

Forward

When a person receives forgiveness of his/her sin and Jesus Christ becomes their personal Savior, they enter into a brand new and very different life style.

As wonderful as they discover the Christian life to be, it is, however, filled with many new challenges. One of these will be an encounter with the enemy of their soul – Satan. No doubt, this on-going attack from Satan will be in ways never before experienced by the new Christian. Therefore, good Biblical guidance on becoming a DAILY victorious follower of Jesus is very, very important!

Sadly, through not understanding the importance of a DAILY walk with the Lord, I have seen many new Christians fall for the traps of Satan. To DAILY follow Jesus is the secret of living a victorious Christian life.

I believe the examples and illustrations that Steve Boyd has included in this book 'So, What Now' will be a tremendous help to any Christian, but especially to new Christians. I highly recommend a copy for yourself and/or a friend.

Tom L. Whidden, founding pastor
Concord First Assembly.

Preface

Making the decision to receive Jesus Christ as personal Savior is the single most important decision any human being can make. That one decision opens for that person the fact that there is absolute truth about the meaning and purpose of life; and how that truth can be experienced today.

A personal relationship with Jesus Christ places a person in the wonderful position of learning about Jesus, not only as Savior, but as Lord also. Jesus as Lord has to do with the quality of life a person lives on this earth. In today's language, it is about making Jesus the President and CEO of your life. Sounds crazy, but Jesus as an active CEO of your life puts you in the position of an incredible adventure we call daily living.

Jesus as Lord provides the opportunity to have a healthy relationship with God Himself, with your own self, and with other people. Although life can be tough, Jesus as Lord is about an abundant life filled with smiles, security and health in the midst of the tough times in our life. That abundant life will produce great power for you in the face the difficulties of life that are certainly there.

Steve Boyd's latest book, <u>So, What Now?</u>, is a wonderful book for teaching practical insights into having a wonderful life once a person receives Jesus as Savior. As you read this book, prepare yourself to think about, meditate on and apply the truths into your life. I suggest you read the book slowly. Have a pen in hand to note the insights that jump out at you. Be patient! God is not done with you. Life with God is not about an event in a building, but a journey every day. <u>So</u>, <u>what</u> are you doing <u>now?</u>

Clayton B. Glickert

One of God's kids daily seeking to make Him Lord.
Former pastor, YAG, Yorktown Heights, New York
Former Assemblies of God district officer, New York
Former President and CEO, Emerge Ministries, Akron Ohio

Presently core group leader of Friends Fellowship, a church for seniors, Syracuse area, New York

Acknowledgements

I would like to express my appreciation to those special people in my life who took time to read my manuscripts and give me feedback to help the accuracy and readability of this book.

First, to Ellen, my wife of 46 years, who is my best friend and closest confidant – whose judgment and suggestions are always God's gift to me.

Dr. Douglas J. Witherup, Executive Director of Ministries, NC Assemblies of God

Dr. William J. Everett, Point of Grace Lutheran Church

Tom L. Whidden, Founding Pastor, Concord First Assembly

Pastor Phil Bennett, Concord First Assembly
Minister of Prayer/Congregational Care

Pastor Clayton B. Glickert, Honorary Presbyter,
New York District, Assemblies of God

William R. Boyd, Point of Grace Lutheran Church

Introduction

In my previous book – "So, Why Jesus" - I was speaking primarily to people who did not have a personal relationship with Jesus Christ and probably were not well versed in the Holy Bible, if they had any knowledge of it at all.

It was my prayer that a person of that background reading that book might find how important and how easy it is to establish a relationship with God through Jesus Christ, and to act to have the assurance that their eternity will be in heaven with all the others who have died with faith in Jesus Christ.

God's grace extends to all of us who put our trust in Jesus Christ. It is by that grace that we are saved, that salvation comes to us, undeserving though we might be. But we must first act to call to Jesus to receive that forgiveness and grace.

Once you have put your trust in Him, you will want to draw closer to Him to enjoy the power and peace that will come out of that relationship. I pray that you will find encouragement in these pages to walk closer to Him and to your fellow Christians.

Note: All *underlining of words* in the following Bible references are my additions for emphasis and do not appear in the Bible referenced.

1

Responding to God

> *Responding to God is simply recognizing from where your blessings and power are derived. - Anonymous*
>
> *It's not my ability but my response to God's ability that counts - Corrie Ten Boom (www.goodreads.com)*

The gift of salvation is free and requires no action on our part to receive it beyond, <u>in faith, accepting it in prayer</u>. Even then, though, we really don't deserve it – we can only receive it - we can't earn it. That is the reason why many people have trouble accepting salvation through grace – it is our human nature to expect to pay for something of great value that we receive. God's grace is incredible, undeserved and free, but it isn't cheap.

First, it did have to be paid for once and for all, and it came at a <u>great</u> price.

Not one of us, though, can do enough good in our life to pay the price for the forgiveness of our sin. No matter how hard we try, we can never earn it. Because we were born with the spirit of sinfulness, that sinful nature has to be put to death first. And we can't do that. Only God can do that, and He has already done it through sending His only begotten Son Jesus Christ to be the atoning sacrifice for all sin for those who receive Him by faith.

Think about how great God the Father's love for us is that he would send His own Son, who knew no sin, to become sin and pay for all sin of all mankind who would trust in Him.

For God so loved the world that he gave his one and only Son, that whoever believes in him shall not perish but have eternal life. (John 3:16 NIV)

Would any of us parents offer our child to be used as a sacrifice for the sake of people who don't have any relationship with us, or don't even know us?

I read a fictitious story involving a man who was the operator of a lift bridge across a river where a daily commuter train traveled, morning and afternoon. He had a young son who loved to visit him in the station house where the controls were located to open and close the bridge. The boy loved to climb down into the machine room below where the massive gears were that opened and closed the bridge. And the father always made sure he was safely back in the control room long before the mechanism was operated.

One afternoon, just before the commuter train was to cross the bridge bringing the commuters out of the city to the stations where they could get off and go home, the bridge had been open for passage of ships. The boy had slipped away to play in the mechanism, unbeknown to the father. The father discovered this just as it was time to close the bridge, and he franticly called his son to come up from below, where, if he stayed, he would certainly be crushed by the gears as the bridge closed. He suddenly heard the sound of the train approaching at full speed, expecting the bridge to be in place for the crossing. If he waited for his son to climb out of the gears, the train would catapult off the open bridge into the river, and hundreds of people would be killed. If he closed the bridge in time for the train to cross, his son would be crushed in the mechanism.

Imagine the horror of realizing that his only choice was to close the bridge and sacrifice his son. He heard the screams of his son as the bridge closed just as the speeding train reached the bridge, but they were drowned out by the noise of the passing train. He saw the passenger cars stream by the windows of his control room. The riders were talking, laughing and drinking – enjoying themselves as they crossed the bridge that was taking them to their home on the other side of the river, unaware of the sacrifice that had just occurred to provide for their safety on that crossing.

Imagine how God the Father must feel as we go through this life enjoying ourselves, focusing on the things that make us comfortable and happy, but ignoring the act of sacrifice that He made as Jesus paid the price to free us from our sin. Our Heavenly Father must cry as He sees how we have ignored His outreach of love. He has provided a bridge across time into eternity, and His son was crushed to close that bridge and make it available to carry us safely across to our home in Heaven.

The sacrifice of Jesus demands a response from us if we are aware of what He did, and why He did it. If we are aware of this, we can't ignore it any more. We must decide now about eternity, for our spirit and soul will live forever – time without end. Heaven or Hell – where will you spend eternity?

The first step is to ask Jesus to come into my heart, to forgive my sin, and to be my Savior and Lord. When I do that, my spirit is reborn with the Spirit of God.

Jesus replied, "Very truly I tell you, no one can see the kingdom of God unless they are born again."

"How can someone be born when they are old?" Nicodemus asked. "Surely they cannot enter a second time into their mother's womb to be born!"

Jesus answered, "Very truly I tell you, no one can enter the kingdom of God unless they are born of water and the Spirit." (John 3:3-5 NIV)

However, this is only the beginning of the new life in Christ. Just as a newborn baby needs to be fed milk for food before he can learn to eat solid food, and he must learn to crawl before he can walk or run, so the new Christian must develop and grow in his/her new life in Christ.

What does it mean to ask him to be Savior and Lord?

A <u>Savior</u> saves us from something that is happening to us or will happen to us. We all were born with a sinful nature that needs to be put to death while we are still alive and can recognize that need. That is what Jesus already accomplished on the cross. If we accept Him as Savior, He will save us from eternal damnation when we enter eternity future. Only He can do that.

A <u>Lord</u> is one who is over us in power and authority. Unlike a 'boss', Jesus as our Lord directs us and protects us from the things of the world that can pull us down. He does only what is best for us because He loves us. He tends to our 'now.' No one could direct your life better, but you must ask Him to assume that role. He still allows us free will to decide for our self.

In the following chapters, I will address some of the ways you can grow in your new life as a Christian so you can eat the solid food of the Word of God, and walk and run in freedom.

I pray that you will be open to the growth He has planned for you. And, if you don't already know Jesus as your personal Savior, that you will accept this wonderful gift of salvation to assure yourself that you will dwell in Heaven for eternity future.

At the end of each chapter, there is a special blank page for you to record any thoughts, observations or action steps that you feel you should remember through ideas that arose from meditating on that chapter. They will probably be promptings from the Spirit of God that you should follow up on right away to grow in your walk.

Act in Faith!

Thoughts, Observations, or Action Steps On Responding to God

2

Prayer Principles

> *"To be a Christian without prayer is no more possible than to be alive without breathing."* - Martin Luther   (www.brainyquotes.com)
>
> *"Prayer is the rope that pulls God and man together. But, it doesn't pull God down to us: It pulls us up to Him."* - Billy Graham
> (www.notesfromthecove.com)

Since Jesus returned to Heaven after His resurrection, He no longer physically walks among us and talks to us in person. But He has left us with a language of communication that He used when He was on this earth, separated from His heavenly Father. Every day, He talked to His Father <u>in prayer</u>.

He modeled for us the way we should live our lives. God the Father is always listening to us and wants us to come to Him in prayer for our joys, our concerns and our sorrows. He doesn't sleep, nor does He focus on more important things. Communication with us is His most important passion. He created us to be His companions for eternity.

We may think our issues are too small or too unimportant to bother Him. We often assume we can do it on our own – we don't need His help. Nothing could be further from the truth. He wants to be involved in every detail of our life, and to offer wisdom and help whenever we call on Him.

You might be thinking, "I don't know how to pray? What should I say? How should I say it? How do I know God heard me? How do I recognize an answer to prayer, especially if it seems like 'no'"?

When Jesus walked on this earth in His brief three-year ministry, He called twelve disciples who traveled with Him all the time. They heard His teaching, they saw His miracles, and they saw Him pray early in the morning. They saw how important His prayer life was, but I don't believe they really understood He was God in the flesh until His resurrection from the grave.

At one time, they asked Jesus <u>how to pray</u>.

Now it came to pass, as He was praying in a certain place, when He ceased, that one of His disciples said to Him, 'Lord, teach us to pray, as John also taught his disciples.'

So He said to them, 'When you pray, say: Our Father in heaven, Hallowed be Your name. Your kingdom come, Your will be done on earth as it is in heaven. Give us day by day our daily bread. And forgive us our sins, for we also forgive everyone who is indebted to us. And do not lead us into temptation, but deliver us from the evil one.' (Luke 11:1-4 NKJV)

This is usually referred to as "The Lord's Prayer", and it certainly was. Some Bible translations precede it with the title "The Model Prayer" (NKJV). Like many of us, I memorized it as a child in Sunday school, and have rotely repeated it hundreds of times in my life.

The way I learned it as a child also had a conclusion (a doxology) that said:

"For thine is the Kingdom, and the Power, and the Glory forever and ever. Amen."

I understand that was added by the church in the Book of Common Prayer because it doesn't appear in any translation of the Bible.

The Lord's Prayer certainly is a beautiful prayer. I personally believe it was intended as a <u>model</u> rather than a <u>rote</u> prayer to be recited, though it is a beautiful prayer just as it is.

There are two parts to the prayer. First, Jesus taught that we should recognize God the Father before we present our concerns or requests:

Our Father in heaven, hallowed be (Holy is) Your name. (May) Your kingdom come (and may) Your will be done on earth as it is in heaven. [my clarifications in parenthesis]

Prayers should be directed to the Father for He is the source of all power and authority and blessing.

Secondly, having praised God the Father with the opening of the prayer, we then present our requests to Him.

Give us this day our daily bread,

Our bread is our daily provision of food and drink that we need for sustenance and health;

And forgive us our sins, as we forgive everyone who is indebted to (has sinned against) us. [my clarification in parenthesis]

We certainly want forgiveness from our sins each day because, even as believers, we continue to sin. And God keeps on forgiving as long as we are sincere in our sorrow for our sins, but we ask it conditionally 'as we forgive others.' If we are withholding forgiveness from someone else, God will not grant us forgiveness. He puts the ball in our court, so to speak.

And do not lead us into temptation, but deliver us from the evil one.

God would never tempt us, nor would he lead us into temptation. Jesus is saying that we should ask the Father to <u>keep us from</u> temptation, and from the lies and deceptions of Satan (the evil one) who is the source of all temptation. God gave us free will to make decisions.

Certainly, these requests are still appropriate for us in this day. But we have many requests that go beyond these three. So, in addition to these requests, or instead of these requests, we talk to our Heavenly Father about what is on our heart – concerns, fears, needs, after we praise him for what He has done for us. He already knows what we fear and what we want and what we need. But He wants us to involve Him in our life so He can show His mercy and grace and wisdom and power that is far beyond anything of ours. Nothing will surprise Him.

Though we address our praise and prayers to God the Father, we ask these things <u>in the name of Jesus</u> who is our Savior. He instructed us to do that:

And I will do whatever you <u>ask in my name</u>, so that the Father may be glorified in the Son. You may ask me for anything <u>in my name</u>, and I will do it.   (John 14:13 NIV)

Prayer is not 'talking to God', as many say, though that is part of it. Rather, it is 'communicating with God.' Communicating involves both <u>talking and listening</u>. If we simply barrage God with our requests without honoring His name and without spending quiet listening to and understanding His reply, we look at God as a genie who should give us whatever we ask for – our 'blessing dispenser.' He doesn't <u>have to</u> grant us any request, though He loves to when we come to Him in humility and thankfulness.

If you are a parent, you know how important it is to you for your children to respect you and honor you as their parent. You teach them how to talk to you and how to come to you when they need something, or when they are happy or sad about something that has happened to them. You want to know what they think, how they feel, what they need as well as what they want. You want to know what they fear, and to help them think through situations that concern them. You have wisdom from your own education and life experiences that they do not yet have, and you want them to benefit from that wisdom rather than make the same mistakes you did. You want them to feel your love and acceptance, no matter what they do or what they experience.

Honor your father and your mother. (Matthew 15:4 NIV)

If you were blessed to have parents who treated you that way (as I did), you know how it feels to have that security in your life. If you didn't, I am truly sorry for you. But nevertheless, you can still understand and have that relationship with your children and give them that sense of security in their life. Let it begin in your family with you.

God the Father is our Heavenly Father. That is the same way He loves us. He wants us to involve Him in our life, to come to Him when we are happy and blessed, as well as when we are concerned or fearful or sad. The big difference from an earthly father is that God knows everything about us - how we feel, what we fear, what makes us happy, what we need and what we want. And he has the provision to make anything available to us that He knows is right for us. His resources are unlimited.

As a loving father, he disciplines us for our own good. His three answers to prayers are "yes", "no" and "not right now." We love to get the "yes" to our request. We hate to get the "no", and we usually see the "not now" as a "no", or we figure that He did not hear or answer us.

Because God loves His children, His answer will be what is best for us, whether we can see it or not. That is what discipline is about – creating in us the character that He desires us to have. He is preparing us for this life and for eternity.

Whoever spares the rod hates their children, but the one who loves their children is careful to discipline them.
(Proverbs 13:24 NIV)

Do we like to be disciplined? Do we see it as punishment, or can we see it as something for our own growth.

Endure hardship as discipline; God is treating you as his children. For what children are not disciplined by their father? If you are not disciplined—and everyone undergoes discipline — then you are not legitimate, not true sons and daughters at all. Moreover, we have all had human fathers who disciplined us and we respected them for it. How much more should we submit to the Father of spirits and live! They disciplined us for a little while as they thought best; but God disciplines us for our good, in order that we may share in his holiness. <u>*No discipline seems pleasant at the time, but painful. Later on, however, it produces*</u>

a harvest of righteousness and peace for those who have been trained by it. *(Hebrews 12:7-11 NIV)*

A fool spurns a parent's discipline, but whoever heeds correction shows prudence. (Proverbs 15:5 NIV)

So often, we don't hear God's answer because we don't take time to listen. Either we get what we ask for right away, or we assume that God didn't hear us or didn't answer us. Yet He is waiting to talk to us.

Does God speak to us in an audible voice? I have never heard an audible voice, though I have met Christians who claim they have heard His voice. I believe they "heard" His voice, not in their ears, but in their heart or their spirit. God is spirit and He created in us a spirit and a soul (mind, will and emotions) to live forever. So it is natural to assume He would communicate with us 'in spirit.' But the effect is as strong as if we heard it with our physical ears.

I have heard Him speak through other people, and to show me an answer through situations that happened in my life. Many times I have seen, with the wisdom of 20/20 hindsight, how God answered me without me seeing it as an answer at the time.

One way He answers us is in the "still small voice" within us – our conscience. When Elijah sought the Lord (1 Kings 19:11-12), he experienced a great wind, an earthquake and fire, but God was not in any of them, though He could have been. He spoke in a whisper.

The LORD said, "Go out and stand on the mountain in the presence of the LORD, for the LORD is about to pass by." Then a great and powerful wind tore the mountains apart and shattered the rocks before the LORD, but the LORD was not in the wind. After the wind there was an earthquake, but the LORD was not in the earthquake. After the earthquake came a fire, but the LORD was not in the fire. And after the fire came a gentle whisper. When Elijah heard it, he pulled his cloak over his face and went out and stood at the mouth of the cave.
(1 Kings 19:11-14 NIV)

And I have learned that when I wait on Him, He gives me that "peace that passes all understanding." Often, after I have waited for a day or two, my request doesn't seem that important to me anymore.

Have you ever asked God for something, and then just sat quietly in silence or sat listening to some peaceful music – maybe reading a book. All of a sudden, a thought comes into your mind that you hadn't had before. Or you hear some words in the music that speaks directly to your situation. Or you read something that speaks to you. You wait for a day or two, and all of a sudden, in the midst of something you're doing, the answer is so clear in your mind. You didn't hear any voice, but you suddenly know the right answer. God speaks to our heart and we know the correct answer to our prayer.

God can work in marvelous ways to communicate with us – He only wants our attention. If we are too busy to listen and the answer is important for us to have, He may allow something to happen to us to slow us down and to get our attention so we can hear to Him.

In Exodus 3, we read the account of Moses. God wanted his attention so he showed him a <u>burning bush</u> that was not consumed by the fire. That would get my attention.

In the Old Testament book of Numbers, Chapter 22, we read of Balak, king of Moab, who summoned Balaam to come to him. God didn't want Balaam to go, but Balaam saddled his donkey and headed off. God put an angel with a sword to stand in his path and block him from going. But Balaam didn't see the angel. However, his donkey did and stopped. Three times Balaam beat his donkey to get him to keep moving on. Eventually, God spoke to Balaam <u>through the donkey</u>.

Then the Lord *opened the donkey's mouth, and it said to Balaam, 'What have I done to you to make you beat me these three times?'. Balaam answered the donkey, 'You have made a fool of me! If only I had a sword in my hand, I would kill you right now.' The donkey said to Balaam, 'Am I not your own donkey, which you have always ridden, to this day? Have I been in the habit of doing this to you?' 'No,' he said.*

Then the LORD opened Balaam's eyes, and he saw the angel of the LORD standing in the road with his sword drawn. So he bowed low and fell facedown. (Numbers 22:28-31 NIV)

Imagine having a dialog with a donkey. That would certainly get my attention. Balaam heard an audible voice, and the donkey's voice saved his life. Of course, it wasn't the donkey's voice, but the voice of the angel making the speech come from the donkey's mouth.

Actually, I think I have had conversations with donkeys (by a different name) but they weren't beasts of burden. And they certainly weren't speaking with the wisdom of God.

Another way that God speaks to us is through <u>dreams and visions</u>. God spoke clearly to Jacob, Joseph, Pharaoh and Nebuchadnezzar in dreams. He confirmed this as a method of His communication to Aaron and Miriam.

Then the LORD came down in a pillar of cloud; he stood at the entrance to the tent and summoned Aaron and Miriam. When the two of them stepped forward, he said, "Listen to my words: When there is a prophet among you, <u>I, the LORD, reveal myself to them in visions, I speak to them in dreams</u>.
(Numbers 12:5-6 NIV)

God confirmed through the prophet Joel this method of communication:

And afterward, I will pour out my Spirit on all people. Your sons and daughters will prophesy, <u>your old men will dream dreams, your young men will see visions</u>. (Joel 2:28 NIV)

I believe that God tries more to talk to us than we do to listen to Him.

The Apostle Paul, in his letter to the church in Philippi, gave this advice that we should all follow today when he said:

Don't worry about anything; instead, pray about everything. Tell God what you need, and thank him for all he has done. Then you will experience God's peace, which exceeds anything we can understand. His peace will guard your hearts and minds as you live in Christ Jesus.   (Philippians 4:6-7 NLT)

The presence of that peace gives you the assurance that God has heard your request and He has everything under control. If we find our self worrying about the issue, we haven't surrendered it to Him.

A pastor once defined <u>worry</u> this way to me:

'Worry is what happens when we take on more responsibility than God intends us to have.'

If you are really seeking an answer from God, pull away from your everyday distractions and find a quiet place to pray. Kneeling has always been the position of serious prayer warriors. I believe it makes you uncomfortable and keeps you from being distracted, but more than that, it shows humility and a submission to God.

But when you pray, go into your room, close the door and pray to your Father, who is unseen. Then your Father, who sees what is done in secret, will reward you.   (Matthew 6:6 NIV)

One very common accompaniment to praying is the act of <u>fasting</u>. To fast means to restrain from eating or drinking. Symbolically, you are saying that your prayer is more important to you than the comfort of your stomach. Some people abstain from food for a day, for a meal, from sweets – whatever in your eating patterns would be a sacrifice for you.

Prayer can be expressed or experienced in so many ways including meditation, reading the Bible, singing or listening to music. Prayer means that you are seeking God's wisdom and direction and blessing in your life.

Many types or categories of prayer have been identified to help understand the many ways we can come to God in prayer. For illustration, I will name and describe <u>four</u> here. They are identified in Scripture in the Apostle Paul's first epistle (letter) to Timothy:

Instructions on Worship

I urge, then, first of all, that <u>requests, prayers, intercession and thanksgiving</u> be made for everyone - for kings and all those in authority, that we may live peaceful and quiet lives in all godliness and holiness. This is good, and pleases God our Savior, who wants all men to be saved and to come to a knowledge of the truth.   (1 Timothy 2:1-4 NIV)

First is a prayer of <u>Requests</u>, also called Supplications or Petitions. It is a prayer of faith. This is a sincere attitude of requesting something important to you that only God can do. It could be for something that you want to do or achieve, such as healing or peace or achieving a closer walk with God. It could be for something that you need or want, either physical or spiritual in nature. One form of this prayer is called 'penitence' which means asking for forgiveness for something we have done that we shouldn't have done, or something we should have done but didn't. Read <u>Psalm 51</u> for an excellent example of this type of prayer.

Therefore I tell you, whatever you ask for in prayer, believe that you have received it, and it will be yours.
(Mark 11:24 NIV)

While Jesus was here on earth, he offered prayers and pleadings, with a loud cry and tears, to the one who could rescue him from death. And God heard his prayers because of his deep reverence for God.   (Hebrews 5:7 NIV)

Secondly, this scripture identifies <u>Prayers</u> meaning a prayer of agreement or consecration or dedication. In this type of prayer, you are asking God's blessing on an event or action such as a baptism, a wedding, or a ministry – for yourself or for another person.

The third category of prayer mentioned in this scripture is one of <u>Intercession</u>. Intercessory prayer is focused on the needs of another person, such as a prayer offered for the healing of another, or for direction or wisdom in their life for a decision they have to make, or for provision for their needs in a difficult time for them. Pastor Jim Cymbala of the Brooklyn Tabernacle says that intercessory prayer is "like touching God with one hand

and touching the other person with the other hand." You are using your relationship with God to reach out for the other person.

Finally, this same scripture mentions prayers of <u>Thanksgiving or Praise</u>. Thanksgiving should always be part of our prayer, no matter what type it is. But a pure prayer of thanksgiving is asking nothing of God, but just expressing praise and adoration to Him for who He is and what He has done in your life – for His majesty and power and glory – for His mercy and grace that you experience in your life. I often do this when I see a beautiful sunrise or sunset, the awesome power of a storm or just sense the deep peace when everything is going so well.

One of the powerful hymns of the church was written by a young Swedish minister around 1886 as he took a two-mile walk in a thunderstorm. It was launched in this country in 1957 through the Billy Graham Crusade and is known around the world today. The hymn, named "How Great Thou Art", starts this way:

> "O Lord my God, When I in awesome wonder,
> Consider all the worlds Thy Hands have made;
>
> I see the stars, I hear the rolling thunder,
> Thy power throughout the universe displayed.
>
> Then sings my soul, My Savior God, to Thee,
> How great Thou art, How great Thou art.
> Then sings my soul, My Savior God, to Thee,
> How great Thou art, How great Thou art!"

That is a prayer of Thanksgiving that has been put to music, and we can pray that by singing it also. Nothing is being asked for. There are so many things in life we enjoy and take for granted, but we should always feel this way about God's generous provision for us.

Another form of prayer that my wife and I have learned could be called <u>Praying Scripture.</u> There are so many promises in scripture and God is faithful – He does not promise something that He will not do. So if a particular scripture really speaks to a need in my life, I will recite that scripture, personalizing it to remind God what He has promised me. He hasn't forgotten, but

He wants to know that we know what He has promised. Here is an example of a prayer when I am trying to do something that I'm not sure I can do by myself:

Scripture: ***For I can do everything through Christ, who gives me strength.   (Philippians 4:13 NLT)***

My Prayer: "Thank you, Lord, for helping me do this because your Word promises me that I can do everything through Christ who gives me strength. I need your wisdom and strength and help to do this correctly."

This is why we need to know what the Scriptures say, to know what promises are there for us to call upon when we need them.

If you don't know what to pray, ask the Holy Spirit to fill you and pray through you. He will use your voice, but will fill your mouth with words or sounds that you will not understand. This is a gift of the Holy Spirit that is exercised in Pentecostal, Holy Spirit-filled assemblies. He knows what to say for you. This is <u>Praying in the Spirit</u>.

That is what happened in the upper room as the apostles waited for the promised Holy Spirit. Read Acts Chapter 2. If this happens in an assembly of Spirit-filled believers, another person will be given the gift of Interpretation, and will be able to put into English what has been said. If you experience this, don't be afraid of it. God's Holy Spirit is operating in that assembly.

The name for this experience is 'glossolalia' – from two Greek words meaning 'tongue' and 'speaking.' Hence the expression "speaking in tongues." There is a prayer language in tongues for public worship (some receive that gift) and there is one for your own personal edification. Ask the Holy Spirit for your prayer language that your prayer life would be more effective.

A discipline that many people use to keep track of their prayer requests and the answers to those prayers is called <u>journaling</u>.

Using any kind of notebook or electronic file, each prayer request is recorded with the date of the request. When an answer is received, that is also recorded with the date. That person can look back over the record of requests and answers and see how God has answered, both in how and when He answered.

Journals can also include thoughts that come to you as you read the word or pray or speak with other Christians. It is your record of what is going on in your life at that time that you want to record for later reference.

Is there a 'right time' or 'best time' to pray? Really, whenever you feel the need to communicate with God, that is a 'right time'. Whenever you are faced with a situation that blesses you, or concerns you, or causes you to wonder what to do, that is a 'right time' to pray. These I would categorize as reactive or spontaneous prayers. Anytime is the right time. But there are also a few times each day that you should plan to pray – being more proactive than reactive.

First, if you want your day to start with God's blessing and direction, it would be good to pray first thing when you get up and begin your day. Early morning prayer gives you the 'edge' by which you have put Satan on alert that you are expecting God to guide you throughout the day. Early morning prayer lets you start the day with God before the interruptions begin to vie for you time.

My wife and I were introduced to this important aspect of prayer when evangelist Bob Bosworth came to our church quite a number of years ago and witnessed how powerful this can be in directing the course of the day. He shared how it had totally awakened a church he had started in South Africa, and to demonstrate the power of early morning prayer to us, he challenged the church to come to a 5:30 a.m. service for a week. Each morning, at 5:30, we were there with our small children, after which I went to work. If affected us so strongly that my wife and I still start the day this way coupled with Bible study, some 30+ years later.

How did Jesus start His day when He was on this earth?

***Very early in the morning**, while it was still dark, Jesus got up, left the house and went off to a solitary place, where he prayed. (Mark 1:35 NIV1984)*

If He knew how important it was to start the day by drawing close to His Father, and <u>He is God</u>, should it be any different for us?

When a couple starts the day together in agreement, they are stronger as a cord of two strands. When Jesus is invited in through prayer and study, He is the third strand of that cord.

Though one may be overpowered, two can defend themselves. A cord of three strands is not quickly broken.
(Ecclesiastes 4:12   NIV1984)

That is part of the reason that my wife and I have been together for 46 years, and we praise Him for his faithful partnership with us.

<u>Secondly</u>, it would be good to 'plan' prayer each day prior to each meal. We are so blessed with the abundance of food we have available to us all the time. There are many areas of the world where food is scarce, where people are fortunate to get one good meal a day. We shouldn't take for granted that this food is there. It is God blessing us each time we can enjoy food and water for sustenance and health. Our prayer prior to the meal recognizes that it is by God's provision that we are able to eat that meal. But, secondly, we want Him to bless that meal that it will be healthy and good for us. There are so many times we hear of people getting sick or even dying from poisoning that came from germs in food they have bought. When God blesses it, He <u>sanctifies</u> it – sets it apart as healthy nourishment for our bodies.

<u>Thirdly</u>, just as we start the day anticipating God's leading and direction as we petition Him in prayer, it would be smart to also reflect at the close of the day as we prepare to sleep. However things have gone that day, as we go to sleep, if we are carrying any anger or unforgiveness or worry, it has been shown that our subconscious mind will process that while our conscious mind rests. That's why we so often have restless sleep and challenging dreams. And we wake up thinking about those things we took with us to bed.

This is a great time to once again petition God and ask Him to take our thoughts and replace them with peaceful, healthy thoughts so that we might sleep well. If you have the awareness that you have offended anyone or you are carrying any anger, ask God for forgiveness that you would be released from that burden and can rest well.

And when you stand praying, if you hold anything against anyone, forgive him, so that your Father in heaven may forgive you your sins.   (Mark 11:25 NIV1984)

If we confess our sins, he is faithful and just and will forgive us our sins and purify us from all unrighteousness. If we claim we have not sinned, we make him out to be a liar and his word has no place in our lives.   (1 John 1:9-10 NIV1984)

All the aspects of prayer that I have discussed are directly focused on **personal** prayer. Another very important dimension of prayer is that which happens when believers gather together and pray together. This **corporate** prayer can be in small sharing groups, in family groups, in ministry groups or in church gatherings. When multiple believers gather together with a particular focus, there is power greater than that available to just the individual. We draw power from one another. We draw encouragement from one another. The author of Hebrews recognized this as he wrote:

Let us not give up meeting together, as some are in the habit of doing, but let us encourage one another—and all the more as you see the Day approaching.   (Hebrews 10:25 NIV1984)

I use most of the DVD teaching materials created by the Brooklyn Tabernacle under the leadership of Pastor Jim Cymbala. There are so many great witness stories shared by members of that congregation and powerful teaching by Pastor Cymbala. The Brooklyn Tabernacle Choir under the direction of his wife Carol, is an incredible blessing to watch and to listen to on these DVD's.

The most amazing focus of that church that I personally have not seen anywhere else is their concentration on prayer. Each Tuesday night, over 1,500 members come to the church just to pray, and that, according to Pastor Cymbala, is the power that drives that church. Doesn't that make sense? If you want to operate with the power of the Holy Spirit, you need to invite Him to operate there as He sees fit. And that is just what is happening in that church. What would happen if all Christian churches sought that power?

The bottom line of this whole chapter is to say that God wants us to call on Him, however we do that, and He has promised to answer us in a way that is best for us. Accept His method and His timing, and you will be blessed.

Thoughts, Observations, or Action Steps on Prayer Principles

3

Bible Blessings

"Education is useless without the Bible." – Daniel Webster

"I am sorry for men who do not read the Bible every day. I wonder why they deprive themselves of the strength and pleasure." – Woodrow Wilson
(www.turnbacktogod.com)

Study: *application of the mind to the acquisition of knowledge, as by reading, investigation, or reflection.* (Dictionary.com)

At times in our lives we have all had the need to acquire additional knowledge to satisfy a desire or a need. It may have been a user's manual for a car or an appliance to understand how to use a feature, or a class in school, college or work where we needed to learn a new discipline. It could have been a hobby or interest where our motivation was just our curiosity to know more. Sometimes our study was enjoyable and sometimes it was frustrating, depending on our motivation. But we have all been involved with study in some way.

Do your best to present yourself to God as one approved, a worker who does not need to be ashamed and who correctly handles the word of truth. (2 Timothy 2:15 NIV)

The Word of God – the Holy Bible – should be a course of study for every professing Christian. I covered it in detail in "So, Why Jesus?" but let me summarize the importance of the Bible to us as believers.

The Bible is a collection of 66 books written by about 40 authors over a period of about 1500 years. Men were chosen by God and given instruction on what to write by God's Holy Spirit. God wants us to know Him and know what He expects of us, and what He has promised to us if we believe in Him. So he had mortal men record His thoughts and instructions for mortal men to read in a language they could understand.

There are two major divisions in the Bible – the Word of God. There is an <u>Old Testament</u> and a <u>New Testament</u>.

The **Old Testament** is a collection of 39 books that tell about God's creation of time, the heavens, the earth, the plants and animals that inhabit the earth, and His most prized creation – mankind. They tell of his judgments against the rebellious nature of man and how He chose a special people through Jacob who was renamed Israel. They tell of His struggle with the nation of Israel to live in accordance with His laws and regulations. Through all their feasts, fasts, festivals, and sacrifices of animal blood to cover the sins of man, they could not break from their sinful nature, and the price for the forgiveness of their sin could not be met by their actions. Finally, God decided to send the promised Messiah to deliver them. He sent His own son Jesus for that purpose.

For God loved the world so much that he gave his one and only Son, so that everyone who believes in him will not perish but have eternal life. (John 3:16 NLT)

Jesus' coming to this earth fulfilled the Law of Moses by which Israel lived – the Law was fulfilled once and for all. A new covenant of Grace was established to free mankind from their sinful nature. For those who recognized Jesus as their Messiah, salvation from the punishment for their sinful nature could be achieved by trusting in Jesus and asking for forgiveness.

The new covenant – a <u>covenant of Grace</u> instead of Law – was established. The Law wasn't eliminated – it is still the Law today.

But as followers of Christ, we no longer will be judged according to the law, but rather, by our faith in Jesus Christ as our Savior – our Messiah. We don't have to celebrate the feasts and festivals because they are not part of the new covenant, except the Sabbath rest on the seventh day.

The books of the Old Testament were written in Hebrew and in Aramaic. Jesus spoke in the Aramaic language.

The **New Testament** is a collection of 27 books that tell the story of that new covenant beginning with the birth of the Messiah – Jesus – and at age 30, His ministry which lasted on this earth for only three years until He was crucified by those who feared Him. They could not eliminate him because He was God, but His three-day death was the plan of the Father. His blood was shed in accordance with the plan of the Father that there would be atonement for the sin of all mankind.

After three days in the tomb, Jesus overcame the grave and arose. He appeared to many, then ascended back to Heaven from where He came, to sit at the right hand of God the Father. He went to prepare a home in eternity for us who have put our faith in Him. And He will be coming back for us as He promised to take us to Heaven to be with Him and God the Father for eternity – time without end. But He sent His Holy Spirit to live within us and to teach from within us so we would have the power to live as we needed to do.

Do not let your hearts be troubled. Trust in God; trust also in me. In my Father's house are many rooms; if it were not so, I would have told you. I am going there to prepare a place for you. And if I go and prepare a place for you, I will come back and take you to be with me that you also may be where I am. (John 14:1-3 NIV1984)

How do we know what God expects of us as we live in this life and wait for the coming of Christ to take us to our home in Heaven?

How do we deal with other people in a way that honors God?

What do we do with the authorities who have been put in place over us?

All the answers to life for us are contained in the Holy Bible if we can read and understand it. The problem for us is <u>understanding</u> the Word and applying it in our life.

There have been many translations of the Bible over the past four hundred years since King James commissioned the writing of the translation called the King James Version, written in 1611. That was the language of the common man of England at that time, but so many of the words have disappeared and are not familiar to us today. More modern translations have been completed for dozens of languages, but particularly in English that we might read and understand it.

There are several modern English translations that make reading it quite easy. For example, you can study the New International Version (NIV), New American Standard Bible (NASB), New Living Translation (NLT), Contemporary English Bible (CEB), Good News Translation (GNT), English Standard Version (ESV), and New King James Version (NKJV), to name just a few.

But here is the catch. Just being able to read the Bible in a modern English version doesn't necessarily mean that you will get the full or correct interpretation. Here's a truth about the Bible that makes it different than any other publication you can read in the modern English language.

Though there were about forty different authors of the 66 books of the Bible, they were really more scribes than authors. The Bible speaks for itself in saying that the Holy Spirit was the author of all the Bible, and He spoke to and through the men chosen by God to "author" the various books. Their thoughts were not just random ideas these men had, but thoughts that the Holy Spirit gave them. You can read the Scriptures and get ideas and understandings, and some will be accurate. But some readers will miss the real meaning that God intended us to have.

<u>All Scripture is God-breathed</u>** **and is useful for teaching, rebuking, correcting and training in righteousness, so that the man of God may be thoroughly equipped for every good work. (2 Timothy 3:16-17 NIV)

Have you ever had the experience of reading something that someone else wrote and you weren't sure exactly what they were saying? Then you talked to the author who explained it, and suddenly you understood exactly what he was saying.

While reading the Bible, we don't have the luxury of asking Moses or David or Solomon or Paul or James or Luke what specifically they meant in a particular passage. They are all deceased.

However, they wrote what the Holy Spirit inspired them to say.

Above all, you must understand that no prophecy of Scripture came about by the prophet's own interpretation of things. For prophecy never had its origin in the human will, but prophets, though human, spoke from God as they were carried along by the Holy Spirit.   (2 Peter 1: 20-21 NIV)

Remember, God is triune – He exists as three persons – Father, Son (Jesus) and Holy Spirit. One God but three persons. He is the same yesterday, today and tomorrow. He never changes. The same Holy Spirit is alive and well today, and He is the original author of all Scripture.

So you can talk to the Author anytime you want, and He will be happy to interpret for you, since He wrote it. You can invite Him in prayer every time you pick up the Bible to be there to help you understand the real truths that you are reading. Just a simple prayer is needed, such as:

"Holy Spirit, you are the author of all Scripture and I want to really understand what I am reading. Please speak to my heart with understanding as I read. Reveal the truths you want me to understand. I ask this in Jesus' name. Amen"

Wow, how incredible is that to have the Spirit of God helping you to study?

The Bible is called the living Word of God for a very good reason. As you read a particular scripture, you will have a particular understanding at that time. Another time, you will read the same scripture and a different understanding will come to you or something new will come out of it. That's because you are at a different place at that time and something speaks to you where you are. If you have sought understanding from the Holy Spirit,

He will reveal to you what you need to understand at that time in your life.

So, with that information, <u>how</u> do you actually study the Bible? Do you start on page 1 and read straight through? Do you pick books and chapters at random and read? Do you read something from the Old Testament and then jump over to something from the New Testament? Do I get a study guide and follow it?

The answer to all of these questions is 'yes' depending on who you are and what works best for you. First, be sure you have a modern English translation of the Bible so the words will make sense to you as you read. To get a feel for the structure or organization of the Bible overall, look at the **Appendix** in the back of this book. There you will see the books organized by category, but not necessarily in chronological order. In fact, the books of the Bible do not appear in chronological order except where there is a 1st or 2nd or 3rd notation such as 1 John, 2 John and 3 John.

Having secured a readable translation of the Bible, and having decided on a plan on how you will read, find a comfortable place with minimal distractions and start. First, ask the Holy Spirit to guide your reading, then get underway. Some people like to take notes on what they think as a result of what they have read. You may want to keep a small notebook nearby. I like to have a pen and/or a highlighter available to mark the portions of scripture that really speak to me, and that I want to be able to find quickly again. Don't be afraid to mark up your Bible – it's a book.

Many Bibles have footnotes with further explanations to help you understand. Some have cross-references in the center column that point you to other related scriptures.

I use a website to help me in my study as I prepare a message for teaching on a particular topic. The site I use most often is www.biblegateway.com. In a matter of moments, you can access any of a dozen translations and search on a topic, a word, or a particular scripture. This is especially helpful if you are trying to pull together thoughts that span different books of the Bible and you are not sure just where to look.

I also have three translations (KJV, ESV and NLT) of the Bible on my iPhone and iPad which I can access and read at any time in a meeting or during a sermon or teaching.

When I want to just read the Bible, I always use the book rather than the electronic versions, unless I am waiting in the doctor's office and want to read scripture. Then I just pull out my iPhone and read.

There are versions of the Bible available on electronic media such as CD. I have a Zondervan 16-CD audio version of the New Testament in the NIV translation. To make it more accessible and convenient, I downloaded it onto my iPod so I can plug in some earphones and have it read to me by someone with impeccable pronunciation, or I can plug my iPod into my car audio and have the Bible read to me as I drive along. We are so fortunate in this day and age to have so many resources available to us, and all for such reasonable costs. All we really need is the desire to know God through His Word.

While we are talking about Bible study, let me mention a few of the study aids that can help you in your study.

First, every Bible has an **Index** in the front listing the books in their order, and telling the page number on which each book begins. This helps the reader find his/her way through the Bible, and gives you the sequence of the Old and New Testaments.

Many Bibles have a limited **Concordance** in the back which lets you search on a word in the Bible and it will show you all the places that word occurs. There are very large and thorough Concordances such as Strong's where many more occurrences of words are listed. I like to use an online resource like www.biblegateway.com which will let you search on any word in any translation of the Bible and in a split second, every occurrence is shown with a portion of the scripture and the search word is bolded to stand out.

Bible **Commentaries** are books written by theologians who are well-versed in the Scriptures and can explain and interpret what the verses of scripture are saying.

They have studied the Bible at great length and are recognized for their wisdom and understanding. They will also supply background information to put those scriptures in perspective so you can understand the times in which they occurred.

Bible **Encyclopedias** contain articles and definitions to thousands of words and terms used in Scripture. "Entries include full historical references such as date, religious environment, family life, customs, language, and literature. All encyclopedia terms are cross-referenced and linked to the verses where they are found to help understand the full meaning of the word in context to its use in specific verses of the Bible. These online articles, provided by well-known and respected Christian leaders, have been written to help those seeking a greater knowledge of Biblical characters, events and places." (www.BibleStudyTools.com)

A Bible **Dictionary**, like any dictionary, defines words found in Scripture and puts them in context of the particular passage you are referencing. Some word searches include the Hebrew or Greek word from which that word originates.

A **Devotional** is a daily reading prepared by someone who is well-versed in Scripture and using a single scripture, they can give you a focus for the day. It doesn't replace Bible study, but, rather, gives you a quick focus to ponder for that day. It should lead to further study on your part when the time is available to you. One that I use daily is "The Word For You Today" at twfyt@wordforyou.com.

There are many **translations** of the Bible that provide you with alternatives to the language you prefer. There are also **parallel Bibles** that print multiple translations side-by-side in columnar fashion so you can jump back and forth.

Several translations are available on **CD** so you can have someone else read the Bible to you as you are working or driving, or would just like to relax and not have to read.

There are many **websites** for those accustomed to doing their study and work online which can provide all of these tools for you.

There are **Bible apps** available for your phones and iPads which allow you to download various translations of the Bible as well as do searches for words or topics. These electronic versions of the Bible are becoming more and more popular, allowing you to carry your Bible with you in electronic format. I'm seeing pastors and preachers using them for sermons and ceremonies. There is a rack much like a music stand that is made to hold your iPad for just this use.

Most churches have adult **Sunday school classes** where the Bible is taught and discussed. Many pastors teach the Bible in their **sermons**. There are also excellent Bible teachers on **TV**, like Charles Stanley, Dr. David Jeremiah, Kenneth Copeland and John Hagee, to name just a few.

There is some excellent Bible teaching available on **DVD's** prepared by pastors who are great teachers. I use a series of DVD teachings by Pastor Jim Cymbala of the Brooklyn Tabernacle in men's groups and in my jail ministry. My wife uses them in her women's groups as well, and we use them together in our couples groups.

We are so blessed to have so much available to us for study that there is really no excuse not to study. Only laziness or lack of commitment can keep us from discovering the many truths that God has given us in His word.

I encourage you to find what works best for you and just get started. Ask the Holy Spirit to help you to decide what to read and to guide you in your study.

Thoughts, Observations, or Action Steps on Bible Blessings

4

Wonders of Worship

> *"The whole person, with all his senses, with both mind and body, needs to be involved in genuine worship."*   Jerry Kerns
>
> *"God is to be praised with the voice, and the heart should go therewith in holy exultation."*   Charles H. Spurgeon
>
> (www.experiencingworship.com)

Worship is a word that can mean different things to different people. It can be a noun meaning 'reverence' (spiritual) or a verb suggesting action (physical). There are two words used in Christianity that are associated with understanding 'worship' – adoration and veneration.

"<u>Adoration</u> *is the worship and homage that is rightly   offered to God alone. It is the acknowledgement of excellence and perfection of an uncreated, divine person. It is the worship of the Creator that God alone deserves."*
(Wikipedia, Worship in Christianity)

What does Scripture say about adoration of God?

Ascribe to the LORD **the glory due his name; <u>worship the L**ORD **in the splendor of his holiness.**   (Psalm 29:2 NIV)

You shall have no foreign god among you; <u>you shall not worship any god other than me.</u>   (Psalm 81:9 NIV)

<u>Worship the LORD</u> with gladness; come before him with joyful songs. (Psalm 100:2 NIV)

God is spirit, and his worshipers must <u>worship in the Spirit and in truth.</u> (John 4:24 NIV)

[Good Order in Worship] What then shall we say, brothers and sisters? When you come together, each of you has a hymn, or a word of instruction, a revelation, a tongue or an interpretation. Everything must be done so that the church may be built up. (1 Corinthians 4:26 NIV)

"Veneration" means to regard with reverence and respect. Certainly, as Christians, we regard God in this way, and our worship is to show that reverence and respect to Him. However, the term isn't only used in reference to God. It is also used in the church in reference to saints and to any authorities within the church, and that is an entirely different kind of reverence and respect.

Only God deserves our adoration. He deserves it continually. But how do we worship Him? What does He expect from us? Let's look at two aspects of worship – **personal** and **corporate**.

Personal worship includes whatever one does to give worship to God on his or her own which does not involve others. It is that person's individual and private adoration of God which can be expressed through prayer, through reading or study, through music, through journaling, or through meditation. When you are focused on God and His power, His glory, His mercy and grace, and His great generosity toward you, you are worshiping God.

There are many tools available to you to help you in your personal worship. There are Bibles, study guides, music CD's, worship DVD's from individuals and groups, Christian radio and TV programs, books by Christian authors and worship leaders, church websites with streaming video of worship services, and much more.

Corporate worship includes all those things we do to honor and love and thank and praise God in the presence of other believers. This can be prayer or group study or music or times of reflection on the love of God and His great faithfulness to us, or local church services. When God the Father or Jesus the Son or the Holy

Spirit is being lifted up in the assembly of believers, you have corporate worship.

So many opportunities are provided for us to worship. All Christian church services should be times of true worship through music, teaching, prayer and preaching of the Word. The order of the service should invite you into a worship experience in which you feel the presence of God as He is lifted up, as Jesus Christ is praised and the Holy Spirit is invited to direct the flow of the worship. If you have experienced that type of church service, you understand what true worship is. If you haven't, I encourage you to search for it.

Come, let us bow down in worship, let us kneel before the Lord our Maker;   (Psalm 95:6 NIV)

Worship the Lord with gladness; come before him with joyful songs.   (Psalm 100:2 NIV)

Unfortunately, there are many churches today where the service is not led by the Holy Spirit. He is quenched, either for lack of knowledge about who He is and how His only mission is to exalt Jesus Christ, or He is quenched out of fear of how He might direct the service and possibly take the control away from the pastor and church leaders. He is not in operation within that "worship" experience.

Without the presence of the Holy Spirit in a worship experience, it is not true worship. It has been said that the majority of churches in America are dying or dead because the Spirit of God has been quenched and no true worship is occurring. The leadership of the church is just "going through the motions" but with no real power to draw people to experience God. It becomes a kind of false worship. Lost people are not being saved or even hearing that they need to be saved from the judgment to come.

False worship

There are many examples of false worship shown in the Old Testament and in the New Testament.

The Holy Spirit had not been revealed in the times of the Old Testament so He wasn't understood, though He was very much present in all of time and eternity past before time began.

Jesus had not yet come to this earth as Messiah as He did at the start of the New Testament. So He wasn't really understood, though He has always existed. He created everything that has ever been created, and has always been part of the Triune God. But people of the Old Testament understood that there was a true God and they knew they should worship Him and should obey the laws He established with Moses on Mt. Sinai when the Ten Commandments were given along with many more requirements for life as God expected it to be lived.

Daniel was a major prophet of God in the Old Testament and his wisdom and actions clearly pointed to a God who was able to do anything. But King Nebuchadnezzar didn't understand this at first. He had a dream that none of his wise men could interpret, but Daniel was able to reveal the mystery with a wisdom that clearly was from the true God. King Nebuchadnezzar realized that Daniel's God was the true God and declared this:

The king said to Daniel, "Surely your God is the God of gods and the Lord of kings and a revealer of mysteries, for you were able to reveal this mystery." (Daniel 2:47 NIV)

Shadrach, Meshach and Abednego were fellow Hebrew prisoners who had been taken to Egypt along with Daniel. Daniel had them promoted to positions of leadership in the kingdom. King Nebuchadnezzar still didn't understand the falseness of his worship, so he had a statue of gold created that was 90 feet high, and he demanded that everyone would worship it.

As soon as you hear the sound of the horn, flute, zither, lyre, harp, pipe and all kinds of music, you must fall down and worship the image of gold that King Nebuchadnezzar has set up. (Daniel 3:5 NIV)

Shadrach, Meshach and Abednego refused, knowing who the true God was, and they openly worshiped their God. Their refusal to worship the gold statue caused them to be cast into the fiery furnace, but God protected them as Jesus walked among them and kept them from any harm. When King Nebuchadnezzar witnessed how their God had protected them, he discovered his own worship was false and demanded everyone worship the true God. He declared:

Therefore I decree that the people of any nation or language who say anything against the God of Shadrach, Meshach and Abednego be cut into pieces and their houses be turned into piles of rubble, for no other god can save in this way.
(Daniel 3:29 NIV)

Why do so many people create their own gods to worship rather than worshiping the one true God? I found this interesting comment in my daily devotional just as I was writing this part of my book, and it speaks so well to this issue:

"The Israelites were commanded not to make any 'graven image' of God. Why? Because God made us, we didn't make Him. A god you make is a god you can control and make do whatever you wish." (*The Word For You Today, June, July, August 2013, p. 18, Alpharetta, GA*)

Of course, we don't create any false gods anymore, do we? Really? What about sports, celebrities, TV, the Internet, hobbies, our work, pornography, computers, social networks, and …? Don't we often set these up as 'gods' or idols that we worship by giving them our time and money?

How do you spend your time? On what do you spend your discretionary money? How do you use your God-given talents? Are other people being blessed in their life by how you live yours?

Take a look at your calendar and notice how you are spending your time. Look over your check or credit card statement and see where you are spending your money. These will tell you what you worship. Consider how much you have reached out to help others in need. What organizations do you support with donations, or who have you helped with financial contributions? Are you tithing your income to your church?

Do you have disciplined time committed to worshiping God? Are you a true worshipper?

True worship

True worship gives praise and honor to the only true God – Father, Son and Holy Spirit. The worshipper must recognize the Triune God, believing that God the Father is all supreme. He is omnipotent (all powerful), omniscient (all knowing) and omnipresent (everywhere present at the same time). Nothing happens that surprises Him, and nothing is beyond His control. God is spirit, not flesh.

Yet a time is coming and has now come when the true worshipers will worship the Father in the Spirit and in truth, for they are the kind of worshipers the Father seeks. God is spirit, and his worshipers must worship in the Spirit and in truth. (John 4:23-24 NIV)

Jesus the Son is the creator and redeemer of all mankind, His blood was shed for the remission of all sin for all who have put their faith in Him, and He will be the final judge at the Great White Throne judgment as man's time on earth comes to an end. See Revelation 20:11-15.

The Holy Spirit is the comforter and the power of God here on earth. He was sent to earth by Jesus, after His ascension back to heaven, to live <u>within</u> the believers and to give them the power to live in victory over sin. He does not lift himself up, but directs all worship to Jesus. That's why He is present in all true worship.

The Holy Spirit helps believers in the Body of Christ to worship in truth by giving them spiritual gifts to operate more effectively within the Body.

There are different kinds of gifts, but the same Spirit distributes them. There are different kinds of service, but the same Lord. There are different kinds of working, but in all of them and in everyone it is the same God at work. (1 Corinthians 12:4-6 NIV)

He goes on to identify the various gifts that He gives, none of which are for the individual to whom they are given, but collectively for the good of others. When these gifts are in operation within the church, true collective worship can occur.

Now to each one the manifestation of the Spirit is given for the common good. To one there is given through the Spirit a message of wisdom, to another a message of knowledge by means of the same Spirit, to another faith by the same Spirit, to another gifts of healing by that one Spirit, to another miraculous powers, to another prophecy, to another distinguishing between spirits, to another speaking in different kinds of tongues and to still another the interpretation of tongues. All these are the work of one and the same Spirit, and he distributes them to each one, just as he determines.
(1 Corinthians 12: 7-11 NIV)

I am convinced that we are living in perilous times and that God's judgment is upon this nation. We have turned from him and we worship our own worldly desires. We have taken God out of our government, our workplaces, our schools, our homes and our marriages. We have focused on satisfying our personal desires, and have sacrificed millions of our almost-born babies through abortion. We have become proud and arrogant toward God and have lost the desire to worship Him. Why shouldn't He judge us?

We are not living as God intends for us to live. We have been called by God to be a living witness to Him in all that we say and do. We are called to sacrifice our selfish desires and seek instead the things that God desires.

Sacrifice implies giving up something that we have or desire for a cause. Conducting our lives in a way that honors and glorifies Jesus requires giving up some of the things that have only temporal value.

A Living Sacrifice

Therefore, I urge you, brothers and sisters, in view of God's mercy, to offer your bodies as a living sacrifice, holy and pleasing to God—<u>this is your true and proper worship.</u> Do not conform to the pattern of this world, but be transformed by the renewing of your mind. Then you will be able to test and approve what God's will is; his good, pleasing and perfect will.
(Romans 12:1-2 NIV)

Try to imagine what would happen in the Christian church today if every worship service were directed by the Holy Spirit and all the gifts He has intended for the church were in operation within the worship experience. The effects would carry far beyond the worship service into our daily lives. Our national morality would rise up to oppose all of the ungodly actions that we see happening such as abortion, aberrant behavior, dishonesty, abuse, murder, theft, illegal drug usage, and general selfish behaviors. Jesus would be lifted up in our land and His judgment might not be pronounced on this nation.

If you wonder about God's judgment upon America, read a fascinating revelation of what has happened and is happening in our country now as recorded in "The Harbinger", authored by Rabbi Jonathan Cahn (published by FrontLine – ISBN 978-1-61638-610-8). Visit his website www.HopeoftheWorld.org Listen to the DVD "The Isaiah 9:10 Judgment" produced by Joseph Farah through WND Films (ISBN 978-193648819-3). You will be shocked and amazed.

I grew up in upstate New York in the America of the 1940's and 1950's when we were a more innocent nation. I never heard of illegal drugs as I went through school, and almost every family I knew had a father and mother who were there for the kids every day. We had discipline in our family, in our school and in our community.

As a child and as a teen, we respected our elders and officers in uniform. We could trust them to help us if we needed help. As a child in school, if we did something wrong, we were punished there, and then again when we got home. Our parents got married, then they moved in together, and then they had sexual intercourse. As children were born, they stayed together to provide a proper home for the kids, and they brought us to church every Sunday – Sunday school, special services and youth fellowship as teens. The last thing we ever wanted to do was to anger or embarrass our parents. We had a reverent fear of God but knew of His love.

Start children off on the way they should go, and even when they are old they will not turn from it. (Proverbs 22:6 NIV)

I reflect on what a wonderful time that was and wish my grandchildren could experience what I did. My 19-year-old grandson asks me about that time and is intrigued by what I tell him life was like in America at that time. I truly wish he and my other grandchildren could experience that time in our country's history. But it is gone and it will never occur again. They will have to share my memories and those of my peers who can tell the story of what it was like.

Worship, however, can be all that it was and more because I did not have the relationship with Jesus then that I do now, and true worship wasn't for me what it is now. This is the best time of my life in my relationship with Jesus Christ and I can share all of that with them to the degree they are interested.

I pray they will each discover the joy of worshiping the Lord with all their heart and learn to rely on His promises to carry us through the joys and challenges of this life. And I pray that for each of you who read this book and have put your trust in Jesus Christ as Savior and Lord.

Therefore, since we are receiving a kingdom that cannot be shaken, let us be thankful, and so worship God acceptably with reverence and awe, for our God is a consuming fire. (Hebrews 12:28 NIV)

Thoughts, Observations, or Action Steps on Wonders of Worship

5

Fellowship and Fun

> *"Our love to God is measured by our everyday fellowship with others and the love it displays."* - Andrew Murray
>
> *"Fellowship means among other things that we are ready to receive of Christ from others. Other believers minister Christ to me, and I am ready to receive."* - Watchman Nee
>
> *(www.whatchristianswanttotknow.com)*

There are times when we need to be quiet in a one-to-one communication with God to grow in our own personal faith, and to study His Word. But we are also called to be in fellowship with other believers to encourage them, to learn from them, and to be encouraged by them. The best example of this involved the believers after they heard Peter's appeal to be baptized and to pull away from the corruption that surrounded them, as recorded in Acts:

The Fellowship of the Believers

They devoted themselves to the apostles' teaching and to fellowship, to the breaking of bread and to prayer. Everyone was filled with awe at the many wonders and signs performed by the apostles. All the believers were together and had everything in common. They sold property and possessions to give to anyone who had need. Every day they continued to meet together in the temple courts. They broke bread in their homes and ate together with glad and sincere hearts, praising God and enjoying the favor of all the people. And the Lord added to

their number daily those who were being saved.
(Acts 2:42-47 NIV)

That may seem a little extreme in today's society and that type of shared living probably only occurs within cults and communes today. But it serves as a great example of putting our own selfish desires and comforts aside for the needs of others. We certainly can do some of this on a more limited scale as we share from what God has given to us. Just as this can happen in families, it can happen within the Body of Christ.

Share with the Lord's people who are in need. Practice hospitality. (Romans 12:13 NIV)

A lesson that took me time to learn is the concept of <u>stewardship</u> of our finances. There is a natural tendency to look at money we earn or are given as <u>ours</u>. We earned it or it was given to us, so, therefore, it is ours to use as we feel is appropriate – right?

The concept of stewardship says 'no' – it <u>all</u> really belongs to God and He has entrusted it to us to be used as He tells us to use it. It really isn't mine to use selfishly, though I can choose to do that if I wish.

One of the things God has told us is to trust Him to provide for all our <u>needs</u>.

And this same God who takes care of me <u>will supply all your needs</u> from his glorious riches, which have been given to us in Christ Jesus. (Philippians 4:19 NLT)

This doesn't say he will supply everything we <u>want</u>. If we use everything we receive for ourselves, there will be nothing left to help provide for the needs of others when God calls upon us. One of the ways He meets our needs is through other people – He doesn't simply rain down cash from heaven. It is already here on earth in the "hands" of a person or an organization. God moves it as He sees fit.

God will use you to bless other people, just as you can be blessed financially by others. A concept shared with me long ago has stuck in my imagination and helps to demonstrate this.

We, the believers in Christ, are like a pipeline. If you have ever watched water flow in a pipe or hose, it will flow as long as nothing obstructs the flow. But if some obstruction occurs, the water slows or stops flowing and little or nothing comes out. In God's pipeline of blessing, it gets stopped up when a believer starts counting his pennies and is afraid to let go of his finances. If it doesn't flow out, then nothing can flow in. That is why some people don't receive. Some Christians are really "cheapskates" who have never learned the blessing of giving to others, so they complain of their lack or refuse to release any of what God has given to them.

An example of this concept is seen in the Dead Sea between Jordan and Israel. It is the lowest point on the earth. Water constantly flows into it from the Jordan River but it can't flow out. There is no outlet so there is no one "downstream" to benefit from the input to the sea. All the minerals and other sediment carried in the water simply settle out on the bottom of the sea. Water evaporates and leaves the sediment behind. The sea is eight times as salty as the ocean. Animals cannot exist in it. The blessings of the incoming water die in the Dead Sea, hence its name.

So it is with so many believers who haven't allowed their blessings to flow on. They pile up in savings when God intended for some of them to flow through us and bless others. Then the person dies and the estate is given away anyway, but not necessarily to the one(s) God intended to bless with it at the time He intended to do it.

In the Gospel of Luke, we read a story of a farmer who was blessed with more grain than he could handle. Rather than give some to others in need, he wanted to keep it all. Here's what happened.

Then he said, 'This is what I'll do. I will tear down my barns and build bigger ones, and there I will store all my grain and my goods'. (continued)

But God had the last word in this selfish action by the farmer, as seen in verses 20 and 21:

But God said to him, 'You fool! This very night your life will be demanded from you. Then who will get what you have prepared for yourself?' This is how it will be with anyone who stores up things for himself but is not rich toward God.
(Luke 12:18-21 NIV1984)

One of God's ways of testing our faith in Him to provide for our needs is in the concept of **tithing**. Tithing simply means giving the <u>first tenth</u> of everything we receive back to God. If we understand that everything came from Him (no matter how we earned it or got it legally) and it has all been entrusted to us to demonstrate stewardship with God's finances, we see tithing as the blessing in which God entrusts us with 90% of everything He blesses us with. Our experience is that we do better on the 90% than we used to do on almost 100% before we learned to tithe.

Why am I writing so much about <u>finances</u> when the topic of the chapter is <u>fellowship</u>? Simply, it is in Christian fellowship that we learn about the needs of others, and we share our needs as well. It is also where we will see this concept demonstrated in other Christian's lives as a witness to us. And it is in Christian fellowship that we can sometimes find our needs met by others.

Throughout the first five books of the Old Testament (the Torah), we read many times about one of many offerings made to God by the Jewish nation. It was called a **fellowship offering.** It was also called, at times, a peace offering or a thanksgiving offering.

'*In the phrase "fellowship offering," the word translated "fellowship" includes the ideas of health, wholeness, welfare, and peace. It is reflected in the common Jewish greeting "Shalom!" This offering apparently symbolizes peace with God because the worshiper joins in the sacred meal (symbolized sharing a meal with the Lord). A fellowship offering could be voluntary as a special offering of thanks to God or could be given as a result of a vow or as a freewill offering (7:12-26). This offering was given by the thousands at special celebrations when many people joined in the sacred meal (1 Kings 8:63). If a man was too poor to bring a voluntary fellowship offering, he would probably be*

given a share in the offerings of others. (Leviticus 3:1)'
[NIV Bible Commentary]

It was through this fellowship offering that the one who offered it felt at peace with God. It was offered, not as a request for something, but as thanksgiving for all that God had done.

Have you ever noticed how good you feel when you help someone else out and they share their appreciation with you? You feel a peace that you have helped them in their need. And I have always found that God blesses me back in a way I didn't expect. We don't give to get, but we do get as we are willing to give.

Fellowship also is a time of sharing our lives with one another. My wife and I have been blessed over the past forty years with the opportunity to share in the lives of others through small sharing groups within the church.

With a small group of up to ten people meeting on a regular basis, either bi-weekly or monthly, we learn to trust one another and care for the needs of one another.

We pray for each other's needs and share meals, and even vacation time, with each other. When a need or concern arises, we know we can call anyone in the group and they will be there for us. It's really expanded family. We study the Word of God together and learn from each other's sharing. We attend Christian events together and grow in our faith as we share in each other's lives. We truly have a lot of fun together.

I worship in a church that has over one thousand people attending that worship service, and I certainly don't know them all, even though I have been there over twenty years. I do know <u>casually</u> quite a few, and I know <u>well</u> a couple of dozen, but I know <u>intimately</u> 15 or 20 who have shared in my life through sharing groups, Bible study groups, Sunday School classes, or service groups where we have shared our labors together.

I believe God created us to share our lives with one another, not to live in isolation. Fellowship is sharing in the lives of others. There are many challenges in this life as we deal with health, money, relationships, death and the society in which we live. So many people struggle with issues that they have to deal with on their own and would love to have the concern and care of others – especially others who have faced the same challenges.

If you don't already belong to a church where the Spirit of God is alive and working, where lives are being changed as the Word of God is preached, find one. Get involved in some way to encourage your growth, through a Sunday school class, through a small sharing group where there is some accountability, through a Bible teaching class or through active worship. Participate in sharing in the body and blood of Jesus Christ through Holy Communion, and learn to worship God. The Christian life is an exciting one, and it is the only one that has a hope (an expectation) for a glorious future in the presence of Almighty God.

'The communion of saints is the relationship that, according to the belief of Christians, exists between them as people made holy by their link with Christ. This relationship is generally understood to extend not only to those still in earthly life, but also to those who have gone past death to be "at home with the Lord" (2 Corinthians 5:8). Since the word rendered in English as "saints" can mean not only "holy people" but also "holy things", the term communion of saints also applies to the sharing by members of the Church in the holy things of faith, sacraments (especially the Eucharist), and the other spiritual graces and gifts that they have in common.' [Wikipedia Communion (Christian)]

The Eucharist, also known as Holy Communion or The Lord's Supper, is a celebration of Jesus' Last Supper at Passover with his disciples before his arrest and crucifixion. He presented the bread and wine, and told the disciples that these common elements were His body and blood, and that they should celebrate by sharing the elements often in remembrance of Him.

Though the bread and wine are interpreted differently in different denominations of Christians, all agree that they represent Jesus' sacrifice, and that He instructed us to share them often. We celebrate the joy of knowing what Jesus did for us as He is represented in the elements of the communion.

For I received from the Lord what I also passed on to you: The Lord Jesus, on the night he was betrayed, took bread, and when he had given thanks, he broke it and said, "This is my body, which is for you; do this in remembrance of me." In the same way, after supper he took the cup, saying, "This cup is the new covenant in my blood; do this, whenever you drink it, in remembrance of me."   (1 Corinthians 11:23-25 NIV)

This was not just a suggestion that Jesus made, but a commandment He gave to His followers to proclaim His death for our sins, and His victory over death and sin that was about to happen.

Jesus said to them, "Very truly I tell you, unless you eat the flesh of the Son of Man and drink his blood, you have no life in you. Whoever eats my flesh and drinks my blood has eternal life, and I will raise them up at the last day.   (John 6:53-54)

When people participate in communion, they are sharing a sacred and intimate fellowship with God and with each other. And as believers in Christ, we will share it with Him again in Heaven.

And he said to them, "I have eagerly desired to eat this Passover with you before I suffer. For I tell you, I will not eat it again until it finds fulfillment in the kingdom of God." (Luke 22:15-17 NIV)

This communion of saints is available to every believer and should be part of every Christian's life. If you are a believer and haven't experienced this, I encourage you to seek it. It may involve finding a new church and getting into group sharing opportunities. But when you feel it is part of your life, you will feel so blessed. You also will find that a Christian life can be fun. Seek it for yourself.

Thoughts, Observations, or Action Steps on Fellowship and Fun

6

Influencing Others

> *"When you reach out to those in need, do not be surprised if the essential meaning of something occurs."* - Stephen Richards
>
> *"Jesus never says to the poor: 'come find the church', but he says to those of us in the church: 'go into the world and find the poor, hungry, homeless, imprisoned."* - Tony Campolo
>
> *(www.goodreads.com)*

When we really understand and appreciate what a blessing it is to be known by God and loved by God, we realize how truly blessed we are. After all, the Creator of the universe cares about us individually and collectively.

However we came to that realization, someone must have reached out to us to reveal this truth to us. Whether it came from something we read, or from something someone said to us, or a sermon we heard, we have heard the truth and have acted upon it. Someone made the effort to reach out to us or we would not have heard the good news.

How, then, can they call on the one they have not believed in? And how can they believe in the one of whom they have not heard? And how can they hear without someone preaching to them? And how can anyone preach unless they are sent? As it is written: "How beautiful are the feet of those who bring good news!"   (Romans 10:14-16 NIV)

Just as God cares for us and has blessed us, there are many people around us who have not experienced God's blessing or experienced the peace that comes from knowing their Savior Jesus Christ. They are caught up in life with all its challenges and are trying to "make it" on their own.

They feel they have to handle everything by themselves and don't realize there is someone just waiting for them to call out for help. They struggle with health issues, job challenges, the cost of living, relationships, lack of encouragement or direction, or just loneliness. They may be anxious, overwhelmed or even depressed with trying to deal with it all. They are looking for relief, and they need a friend to come alongside them and lend a shoulder or hand, or to share an encouraging comment.

Imagine this situation. You take a friend to the airport and decide to sit for a while, enjoy a cup of coffee and people-watch before going home. You notice a young mother with a toddler who has just come off a flight, and it is clear that she is stressed and confused. You are close enough to hear her and notice that she speaks French. You do also. She tries to get directions but no one else around her can understand and help her. Her frustration is growing.

Either you can just sit there, enjoy your coffee, and watch to see what happens, or you can choose to be the Good Samaritan that she needs. Which would you do?

Now imagine this situation. You know someone who is going through a very difficult time in his or her life. He or she may have experienced a stalemate in their career or they might be dealing with a health crisis, they may have just lost a loved one or dear friend, a child might be in a bad situation, and they have no one close to turn to for help or advice. They seem to have no hope.

They don't know where to turn. You know about the situation, and you are a born-again Christian. You know Jesus as your Lord and Savior, and you know the comfort you receive from reading the Word of God and from praying. You have felt the comfort of the Holy Spirit as He encourages you, and you know the hope of salvation that lies ahead for you. You know exactly what this person needs, or better yet, you know <u>who</u> this person needs.

Will you sit back and enjoy your coffee and watch what happens as this person tries to make sense of what life has dealt them and figures out how to proceed, or will you be the Good Samaritan he or she needs, and introduce him or her to Jesus Christ and offer your help?

This is what Christianity is all about – sharing who we have found for our salvation with others who are lost and in need of a Savior.

I believe most people follow the spiritual leadership of their parents, if there was in fact any direction given. Or, they seek some kind of association with a group who feel they have direction and have found meaning in their lives. Many experiment with different cults and different religions, seeking that sense of belonging.

But, we, as Christians, know that fulfillment in this life and having a true hope for the life that lies ahead of this one can only come from a true relationship with the only true God. That happens when a person comes to the saving knowledge of Jesus Christ who is the Son of God. Jesus said,

"I am the way, the truth and the life. No one comes to the Father except through me." (John 14:6)

They will not find hope for the future in any other religion, because all other religions offer no future hope. The knowledge of true hope will probably come through another person who befriends them and shares this truth.

A ministry that I actively participated in for almost 35 years called Tres Dias (www.tresdias.org) had a simple three-step process to remind us of this call to reach out to others as a minister of the gospel:

1. Make a new friendship with someone you know or meet
2. Become a real friend to that person
3. Introduce that new friend to Jesus Christ.

We don't need any theological training to do this. God doesn't wait to call us until we are already equipped to minister, but he equips those He calls to minister in His name as part of the call. Think about it – if you are already trained to do the ministry and great things happen, who is going to get the glory? You will, of course. But if you have no training but act in faith and confidence in Jesus' leading, and great things happen, who will get the glory? God will!

There was a sign in the lobby of a small church that read: 'Pastors – 1; Ministers – Everyone.' As believers, we are called to spread the good news of salvation through Jesus Christ to everyone we know or meet. If you get rejection, it isn't you they are rejecting – it's the gospel. Pray for them – ask God to soften their heart to receive the good news. I recommend praying for them before you first speak to them, asking the Holy Spirit to go before you and prepare the soil of their heart to be receptive.

I remember the first time I shared Christ with someone who was lost. I was working in a large company and I was used to carrying a small credit card-sized tract or pamphlet called "The Four Spiritual Laws" distributed by Campus Crusade for Christ. I gave a pamphlet to a female coworker with whom I was working, and asked her to take it home that night and read it. I would ask her about it the next day. She read it that night in bed, and had an out-of-body experience right there. I had heard about this type of experience but she was the first to tell me first-hand what it was like. It demonstrated so vividly to me how God's Holy Spirit can work so powerfully without me having to do anything more than be ready to offer a simple pamphlet when He prompted me. Was she anxious to talk to me the next day? Her life really turned around after that because of that initial experience. Do you think that encouraged me to keep sharing? You had better believe it!!

For a few years, I was a corporate trainer and traveled all over the country conducting one-day and two-day communication workshops. I spent hundreds of nights in hotel rooms and every room had a 1611 Old King James Gideon Bible in the drawer. I always wrote and highlighted inside the front cover "Please read John 3:16 and 1 Corinthians 10:9-10." I would then highlight these verses with a yellow highlighter pen, and I would put a copy of "The Four Spiritual Laws" as a marker in the John 3:16 reference as a page marker. I never put my name in it, so no one ever contacted me to say how it might have affected their life. I wasn't looking for recognition – just planting seeds.

Sometimes we plant seeds and sometimes we water seeds that someone else planted. But only God can bring forth the harvest of souls for the Kingdom. (1 Corinthians 3:6-8)

There is a similar pamphlet produced by Billy Graham Evangelistic Association called "Steps to Peace with God." They are available through their website and through the Billy Graham Library in Charlotte, NC.

Each time you share the gospel with someone new, you will become more confident to do it the next time. As people respond to your invitation to receive Christ as Lord and Savior, you will become more convinced that you have been called to minister for Jesus. I have been doing it for over 25 years and have had the honor and privilege of leading more than seventy people to the saving knowledge of Christ.

I have been doing jail ministry for the past seven years and currently conduct a Sunday school lesson each week with a group of teen boys in a nearby state juvenile detention facility. In the adult jail where I shared for five years, I found a diversity of men who were there for reasons ranging from behavioral issues to murder. They were very much aware of their need for a Savior, and many had already received Jesus as Lord and Savior. Many came to that relationship during their incarceration. They were hungry for the Word of God and looked forward to each session. It was a great growth experience for me as I learned to put aside my fears and concentrate on sharing the grace of God.

There are so many ways you can learn to reach out both inside and outside the church. You just have to be willing to step out of your comfort zone and make yourself available. God will use you in ways you can't imagine now. The only 'ability' he wants is your <u>avail</u>ability.

There is such a great satisfaction in knowing you were used to help someone find the truth about their need for salvation, and they will spend an eternity in Heaven partly because of your actions.

Thoughts, Observations, or Action Steps on Influencing Others

7

Seasons of Life

> *"Until the pain of remaining the same hurts more than the pain of change, people prefer to remain the same."*
> - Dr. Richard Dobbins   (www.RDDIM.org)

All previous chapters have focused on living your life as a Christian in a way that will draw you closer to God through your relationship with Jesus Christ. I have shared my own observations on life as drawn from my experiences as I have lived my life and observed others around me as they live out their lives, and as I have read and been taught the Word of God.

I don't read what others have said and then pass that along as research. So if I am wrong in anything that I share, you can fault only me.

Here is what I have observed about life itself as I look at what has happened to me and to others around me, and as I look forward to what lies ahead according to what the Bible tells us.

I see <u>seven seasons</u> that happen to some degree in the life of every person. Not everybody experiences all of them.

Remember that God created time, and His most important creation – mankind – was last. We were created to be companions of God for eternity future, but we have to decide whether we want that for our self. It doesn't just happen automatically.

Creation is that miraculous step that God begins when a man's sperm has fertilized an egg in a woman's womb and cells start to divide and form the unique person you will be for the rest of your life. This event is called conception because a new life has been conceived or begun. Only God can create life within that fertilized egg. The characteristics of that new life come from the DNA of both parents, and God is there to impart that divine spark of life. Life has begun.

For you created my inmost being; you knit me together in my mother's womb. (Psalm 139:13 NIV)

All life is precious to God since He has created it. There are no mistakes and no "illegitimate children", as we so often hear. Each baby is a legitimate created child of God. Only some parents are illegitimate as parents because they are not responsible together for the child that God has created through them.

Transition Into Independent Life occurs when that child has developed in the womb to the point that he is ready to begin to learn how to function on his own outside the womb. Through the process called birth, the connection to the mother is severed, and the little body starts to use its own organs to breath, to pump its own blood, and to learn how to take nourishment to grow and develop. Life began at conception in the womb, but life as a separate independent individual begins at birth. It's a sad note to have to mention that <u>over fifty million</u> babies in America have been deprived of the opportunity to make this transition into independent life because of the horrendous, murderous act of abortion. One of God's Ten Commandments for all mankind says: ***You must not murder.*** *(Exodus 20:13 NLT)*

Development of the mind and body of this new independent person continues after birth for the next twenty or so years. Physical and mental development happens with the experiences that person goes through as he or she functions in life. Habits and preferences develop a unique personality which distinguishes that person from all others on earth. Each person is a unique creation of God.

As you do not know the path of the wind, or how the body is formed in a mother's womb, so you cannot understand the work of God, the Maker of all things.   *(Ecclesiastes 11:5 NIV)*

Apex of Life occurs when the physical development has reached the point where that person is fully formed as God intended. This will probably be in our twenties. We can still continue to develop muscular strength and increase our mental faculties with extra effort, but our body is complete as God has planned it. If we travel up a hill, we eventually reach the apex of the hill when we stop going up and start going down. So it is with life.

Decline begins after the Apex when we start to show signs of wear, when muscles can no longer do what they used to do, and we start to experience aches and pains we didn't use to feel. Our energy is not what it used to be. We slow down a little and choose less stressful activities in which to participate. Often our joints and organs begin to fail. I have lost three major organs and had both knees replaced as a testimony to this truth.

Our body has begun the process of dying. The longer this goes on, the more challenges we will face. There is a gradual loss of hearing, vision, memory and other bodily functions. We lose our teeth, our hair and our muscle and skin tone. Wrinkles appear. We call the start of this time 'middle age', and many have a middle-age crisis as they begin to realize they have reached a turning point in their life that they can't stop. Their body is aging and dying. They are at least half-way through their life.

Transition Out of Life is the final physical step in the cycle of life where this earthly 'tent' called our body has finished its work, and the spirit and soul within us leaves the physical body and moves to a spiritual body. The person is said to have died, but really, he or she has been transitioned from the physical (natural) body into the spiritual body they will have for eternity future.

...it is sown a natural body, it is raised a spiritual body. If there is a natural body, there is also a spiritual body.
(1 Corinthians 15:44 NIV)

Some people believe that when we die, everything just ceases and we are no more. The Bible tells us that only our body dies, but our spirit and soul (mind, will and emotions) go on for eternity. Combined with the new spiritual body, our soul will exist forever, and we will dwell wherever we have prepared to be for eternity.

Everyone comes naked from their mother's womb, and as everyone comes, so they depart. They take nothing from their toil that they can carry in their hand. *(Ecclesiastes 5:15 NIV)*

Re-Creation happens when we die, and will happen when Jesus returns for His church to take his believers to Heaven. The trumpet will sound and we will be caught up in our spiritual body to meet Him in the air. Our resurrection from death is a marvelous re-creation that happens instantaneously. If we are still alive, we will experience the same instantaneous re-creation.

... in a flash, in the twinkling of an eye, at the last trumpet. For the trumpet will sound, the dead will be raised imperishable, and we will be changed. *(1 Corinthians 15:52 NIV)*

God desires for us to be with Him for eternity future, and that is why he made our soul eternal – surviving death of the body. But because sin entered the perfect world He had created, we have inherited that sinful spirit. Only the sacrifice that Jesus made for us on the cross will cleanse us of that sinful nature and make us right for eternity with God, <u>if we have accepted</u> that sacrifice.

When all is finished on this earth and Jesus sits at the Great White Throne to judge all unbelievers, they will be accountable for what they have done with this life. Only if our spirit has been redeemed through our acceptance and faith in the forgiveness of Jesus Christ will our eternity future be in Heaven. Raptured believers will not be there at the Great White Throne Judgment – we will stand before the Judgment Seat of Christ (the Bema Seat) upon our translation at the Rapture, and we will receive our Heavenly rewards for how we have lived our lives. There will be no punishment for our sins. Jesus has already taken that judgment upon himself. If we are <u>not</u> redeemed, our fate will be the lake of fire that was created for Satan and his followers. Read Revelation 20:11-15

One thing can be counted on – if you were transitioned into life (birth), you will be transitioned out of life (death) at a time <u>appointed by God</u>. And at some future time, you will be judged according to your works or by your faith in Jesus Christ.

And as it is appointed for men to die once, but after this the judgment. (Hebrews 9:27 NIV)

There is no such thing as reincarnation. You live only once.

Your eyes saw my unformed body; all the days ordained for me were written in your book before one of them came to be. (Psalm 139:16 NIV)

That Re-Creation to the spiritual body concludes the seasons of life. We are only natural/physical for a brief time, whether that time is measured in hours, days, years or decades. It might be a life of pleasure and joy, or it might be filled with suffering. Most lives will have some of both. God has a purpose in every life, and only when we seek to know Him and follow His plan for us will we have the joy of knowing His peace and assurance.

I have struggled with knowing several people whose life had seemed to have more than a fair amount of suffering, or had ended in what seemed way too short a time. We want to understand why some suffer so much or die so early, especially when they were such a good person. God doesn't have to explain it to us, and He doesn't have to explain His thinking in any circumstance.

He does assure us in His Word that our thoughts are not His thoughts, so to 'understand' why He allows certain things to happen is not for us to know. We should just trust in Him and believe He has a greater purpose in what is happening. He is always in control. Our job is to trust in Him and accept what He has for us.

And we know that God causes everything to work together for the good of those who love God and are called according to his purpose for them.   (Romans 8:28 NLT)

When my sister-in-law was killed in an accident in her mid-twenties, just as she was engaged to be married and was starting her professional career as a lawyer, it made absolutely no sense to us why God would allow this to happen. She loved the Lord and she loved people. She had some serious medical issues that could have restricted her life some, but she always overcame, until this time. A scripture we found that gave some comfort says:

Good people pass away; the godly often die before their time. But no one seems to care or wonder why. No one seems to understand that God is protecting them from the evil to come. (Isaiah 57:1 NIV)

No one really knows what lies ahead in their physical life. If we did, we would probably panic and act irrationally, and perhaps distance our self from God. Our life is finite – everyone has a beginning and an end. Only God knows what those limits are for each of us. He has a plan - everything is under His control.

As life begins to fade into the senior "golden" years, and physical problems associated with aging may put us in hospitals and nursing homes, it can be a very lonely time, especially if we are alone. Even if living at home or in assisted care with others around, we tend to focus on our failing health. We see others around us suffering and dying. Without a really strong faith, it can be hard to see God working in all of this, even though His word tells us that He is. So many conditions just seem to worsen with time. Many people can start to lose hope to carry on.

Everyone needs to have a sense of hope that life is leading to something, no matter what we are going through. Many say they have no hope, and for many, that is true. For someone who does not have a relationship with God through Jesus Christ, I don't know what hope they can have beyond death.

Hoping is not wishing – hope has an <u>expectation</u> of something coming. If you are a Christian, your glorious hope is in your salvation. When you put your faith in Jesus Christ, your eternity future (time without end) will be in the presence of Father, Son and Holy Spirit in the New Heaven. If you haven't put your faith in Jesus, your only expectation is an eternity of suffering in hell. No one should have that "hope", but it should be expected.

Now faith is the substance of things hoped for, the evidence of things not seen. (Hebrews 11:1 NIV)

A few people have had a glimpse of Heaven in a near-death experience, but most Christians have never seen Heaven. Yet we know by faith that it is real and we will be there someday.
No matter what we are experiencing, that hope has to carry us through. The Apostle Paul faced many near-death experiences but his proclamation was:

To live is Christ, but to die is gain. (Philippians 1:21 NIV)

Paul looked forward to transitioning to his spiritual body so he could be with God the Father and with Jesus Christ. Yet he recognized that each day he was experiencing Jesus working in every situation of his life. That is how we as Christians can also be.

In an earlier chapter on Influencing Others, I encouraged you to extend your faith to others around you. If you consider this aspect of the Seasons of Life, think about others around you who might be all alone without hope. Whether they are in hospitals, nursing homes, hospice houses, jails or just living alone – let your light shine in their lives and give them hope to go on. Help them to negotiate through their seasons of life. Introduce them to Jesus and the hope of salvation they can have to carry them through.

Thoughts, Observations, or Action Steps on Seasons of Life

8

Just In Case (Conclusion)

As I conclude this book, I'm reminded that the basic premise for writing it was to encourage those who are new to the Christian faith to grow in that faith and to draw closer to Jesus. If that is you, I hope you have been encouraged by what I have presented in these pages.

I must also allow that someone might read this who really doesn't have a personal relationship with Jesus Christ as Savior and Lord. So, Just In Case, let me repeat here what you need to do to establish that relationship, to be forgiven of your sins, and to be assured that your name is written in the Lamb's Book of Life, and that your eternity future will be in Heaven.

The steps are outlined at the end of this book after the Appendix on a page entitled **Steps to Salvation**. If you haven't done this already, please do this while you still have the option to make that decision. There are no guarantees to the number of days we each will have left on this earth, and only while we are alive here can we decide where our eternity future will be. Decide now. Not to decide is to decide because the sinful nature you were born with will take you into an eternity of suffering in the lake of fire unless you turn to Jesus for forgiveness.

May God bless you as you grow in your faith and await the return of Jesus to usher us into eternity with Father, Son and Holy Spirit in Heaven. I can't adequately communicate what an exciting life it is to be following the leading of the Holy Spirit as you go through each day. God loves you and has an exciting plan for your life if you seek Him with all your heart. Place your trust in Jesus – He will not let you down. He will be your peace.

Christianity is an exciting life through which you can discover the great joy of knowing that the God of the Universe knows you personally and cares about you, and that He wants you to be with Him for eternity. He wants to walk with you each day in both your joys and your sorrows, and to help you overcome the challenges of this mortal life. He gives you blessed hope for what lies ahead in your eternity in Heaven. Rest in His love.

If you wish to contact me about anything I have shared in this book, you can email me at **whatnowreply@yahoo.com** and I will reply as quickly as I can. Leave me contact information and your comment or request so I know the nature of your contact. Thanks for reading this book – I hope it has encouraged you in your faith.

Shalom!

Appendix

Categories of Books of the Old Testament

<u>Books of the Law</u>: The Pentateuch

- Genesis, Exodus, Leviticus, Numbers, Deuteronomy

<u>Books of History</u>: The Historical Books

- Joshua, Judges, Ruth, 1 & 2 Samuel, 1 & 2 Kings, 1 & 2 Chronicles, Ezra, Nehemiah, Esther

<u>Books of Poetry and Wisdom</u>:

- Job, Psalms, Proverbs, Ecclesiastes, Song of Solomon, Lamentations

<u>Books of Prophecy</u>:

- <u>Major Prophets</u>: Isaiah, Jeremiah, Ezekiel, Daniel

- <u>Minor Prophets</u>: Hosea, Joel, Amos, Obadiah, Jonah, Micah, Nahum, Habakkuk, Zephaniah, Haggai, Zechariah, Malachi

Categories of Books of the New Testament

<u>The Gospels</u> (the Good News)

- Matthew, Mark, Luke, John

<u>Book of History (of the church)</u>:

- Acts (of the Apostles)

Paul's Letters to the Churches:

- Romans
- 1 & 2 Corinthians
- Galatians
- Ephesians
- Philippians
- Colossians
- 1 & 2 Thessalonians
- 1 & 2 Timothy
- Titus
- Philemon

General Letters

- Hebrews
- James
- 1 & 2 Peter
- 1, 2 & 3 John
- Jude

Apocalypse, Letters to Churches, and Prophecy

- Revelation

Steps to Salvation

First, in prayer, you have to admit to God that you are a sinner. *(Romans 3:22-24)*

Second, you must ask Jesus Christ to forgive your sins by His sacrifice. *(1 John 1:8-10)*

Third, you need to ask Jesus Christ to come into your life as your Savior and your Lord. Commit your life to Him and commit to following His ways.

Here again is a sample prayer you can pray to invite Jesus Christ into your life:

Heavenly Father, I know that I am a sinner because your Word tells me that. I want to be free of the guilt of my sin.

Jesus, I know that you came to this world to pay the price for the forgiveness of my sin. I ask you now to forgive my sin, and to be my Savior and Lord. I want to serve you for the rest of my life.

Holy Spirit, I need your power to live the Christian life. Please fill me now with your power.

I thank you, God, for your grace and mercy, and for saving my soul, in Jesus' name.   Amen

---

I prayed this prayer and received Jesus as my Savior and Lord today. My sins are forgiven! I'm ready for eternity with you Lord!

_____

Date: ___/___/____

If we claim to be without sin, we deceive ourselves and the truth is not in us. If we confess our sins, he is faithful and just and will forgive us our sins and purify us from all unrighteousness. (1 John 1:8- NIV)

*If you declare with your mouth, 'Jesus is Lord,' and believe in your heart that God raised him from the dead, you will be saved. For it is with your heart that you believe and are justified, and it is with your mouth that you profess your faith and are saved.
(Romans 10:9-10 NIV)*

*Jesus answered, 'I am the way and the truth and the life. No one comes to the Father except through me.'
(John 14:6 NIV)*

I tell you that in the same way there will be more rejoicing in heaven over one sinner who repents than over ninety-nine righteous persons who do not need to repent. (Luke 15:7 NIV)

Everyone who calls on the name of the Lord will be saved. (Romans 10:13 NIV)

*Therefore, since we have been justified through faith, we have peace with God through our Lord Jesus Christ.
(Romans 5:1 NIV)*

*Yet to all who did receive him, to those who believed in his name, he gave the right to become children of God.
(John 1:12 NIV)*

And the peace of God, which transcends all understanding, will guard your hearts and your minds in Christ Jesus. (Philippians 4:7 NIV)

Bibliography

Websites referenced:

    www.BibleGateway.com
    www.Wikipedia.comzzzZ
    www.BibleStudyTools.com
    www.Dictionary.com
    www.HopeoftheWorld.net
    www.brooklyntabernacle.com
    www.tresdias.org
    www.goodreeds.com
    www.brainyquote.com
    www.notesfromthecove.com
    www.turnbacktogod.com
    www.experiencingworship.com
    www.whatchristianswanttoknow.com
    www.RDDIM.org
    www.freedigitalphotos.net

The Word For You Today, Alpharetta, GA
June, July, August edition, 2013, twfyt@wordforyou.com

"The Harbinger" - Rabbi Jonathan Cahn,
  Published by FrontLine, ISBN 978-1-61638-610-8

"The Isaiah 9:10 Judgment" - Rabbi Jonathan Cahn
  DVD   WND Films, produced by Joseph Farah
     ISBN 978-193648819-3

Cover photograph and title page graphic purchased from
www.freedigitalphotos.net.

THE HOLY BIBLE, NEW INTERNATIONAL VERSION®, NIV®
Copyright © 1973, 1978, 1984, 2011 by Biblica, Inc.® Used by permission of Zondervan*. All rights reserved worldwide. www.zondervan.com. The "NIV" and "New International Version" are trademarks registered in the United States Patent Office by Biblica, Int.

THE HOLY BIBLE, NEW LIVING TRANSLATION, NLT
Scripture quotations are taken from the *Holy Bible*, New Living Translation, copyright ©1996, 2004, 2007, 2013 by Tyndale House Foundation. Used by permission of Tyndale House Publishers, Inc., Carol Stream, Illinois 60188*. All rights reserved.

referenced in accordance with Fair Use Guidelines

Made in the USA
Columbia, SC
30 November 2023